— BALI —

The Journey in Heaven on Earth

This book is dedicated to
my mother, Budhieningsih Sudono
and father, Chandra Kemal,
family members
and friends.

Sanctions Violations of Article 113

Act No. 28 of 2014 about Copyright

(1) Any person who with no economic rights infringes referred to in Article 9 paragraph (1) letter i to use commercially shall be punished with imprisonment of 1 (one) year and / or a maximum fine of Rp 100.000.000 (one hundred million rupiah).

(2) Any person who with no rights and/or without permission of the Author or Copyright owner infringes the economical right of the creator as referred to in Article 9 paragraph (1) letter c, d, f, and / or h to Use It commercially shall be punished with the imprisonment of 3 (three) years and / or a fine of Rp 500,000,000.00 (five hundred million rupiah).

(3) Any person who with no rights and / or without permission of the Author or Copyright owner infringes the economical right of the creator as referred to in Article 9 paragraph (1) letter a, b, e, and/or the letter g to use it commercially shall be punished with imprisonment of 4 (four) years and/or a maximum fine of Rp 1.000.000.000 (one billion rupiah).

(4) Any person who meets the elements referred to in paragraph which are carried out in the form of piracy, shall be punished with imprisonment of ten (10) years and/or a maximum fine of Rp 4.000.000.000 (four billion rupiah).

— BALI —

The Journey in Heaven on Earth

Written and Illustrated by **Indah P.**

Foreword by **Putu Fajar Arcana**

KOMPAS
PENERBIT BUKU

BALI
The Journey in
Heaven on Earth

First Published in 2020
by Penerbit Buku Kompas
PT Kompas Media Nusantara
Jalan Palmerah Selatan 26-28,
Jakarta 10270
e-mail: buku@kompas.com

Illustrations: Indah P
Cover Design: A Novi Rahmawanta

xx + 100 pages.; 14 x 21 cm
ISBN 978-623-241-204-0
ISBN 978-623-241-203-3 (PDF)
KMN 582013004

Printed by PT Gramedia, Jakarta.
The printer is not responsible for the content of this publication

Contents

Foreword

The Lingering Impression of Memory

Putu Fajar Arcana

Not only does Bali imprint upon you in memories, she also puts many artists and researchers to the task of exploring her; peeling away layer by layer until they arrive at the core of her singularity and beauty. The profound memories left by such people often find form in vivid snapshots and printed work. These published works in turn inspire so many more people to live out their own experiences on this small island east of Java.

In her book *Eat Pray Love* (2006), celebrated author Elizabeth Gilbert penned a romantic rendering of her memories there. After a snaking journey through Italy and India to celebrate the abundance of food and a crestless wave of spirituality, it was in Bali that Gilbert finally rediscovered love. The story, which had already touched so many people from around the world, became even more popular when it was made into a movie of the same name and played by the illustrious Hollywood actress Julia Roberts. The movie sparked such excitement that then-tourism and culture minister Jero Wacik even felt the need to visit the location where it was being filmed.

Gilbert depicts Bali as a wellspring of knowledge and beauty that guided her back to love. Before embarking on her long journey to the Island of the Gods, Gilbert's story was one of hardship framed by divorce. Such a predicament inevitably feeds into Bali's liveliness and allure to travelers, whatever their intent. Bali turns into an ideal place that promises happy memories for anyone willing to set foot on the island and turn over every rock.

Indeed, long before Gilbert started wrestling with her own restlessness, Scottish American Muriel Stuart Walker (1898-1997) found herself in a quandary after watching *Bali: The Last Paradise* on Hollywood Boulevard. Muriel decided the very next day to go to Bali in search of the last heaven on earth.

The decision she made in 1932 would dramatically change Muriel's life. After landing in Batavia, she bought herself a car and set a course to Bali and told herself, wherever she finds herself when the car runs out of gas, that is where she would stay. Surely enough, one day her car quit right in front of a *gapura* (an ornamental gate), which she thought was a temple. On her way in, she was welcomed by the king of Klungkung, who would later raise her as his fourth child and named her K'tut Tantri.

Muriel was not just a lonely traveler, she was one of Hollywood's best screenwriters in the 1930s. She would later be known for her memoir *Revolt in Paradise*, which was translated into the Indonesian, *Revolusi di Nusa Damai*. We now know that this book had inspired so many people from America and around the world to visit Bali in droves. In the 1970s, Bali was inundated by wave after wave of wandering, pot-smoking hippies looking for a piece of paradise around Kuta and Legian. The phenomenon had caused trouble for so many people and even split public opinion in two, precisely at a time when Bali was trying to pioneer a modern tourism industry.

This narrative extends to other big names like Miguel Covarrubias, the Mexican artist based in America who wrote *The Island of Bali* (1937) after an inspired visit. There is also the eminent German photographer Gregor Krause, who published a book titled *Bali 1912* (1920). This book contains hundreds of photos on the exotic lives of Balinese women at the time; no doubt it has drawn the attention of many painters and photographers to Bali.

The arrival of researchers and artistic types was welcomed by the Dutch colonial government, which had launched a program called *Baliseering* or "Balinization". In the late 1920s, Dutch Orientalists felt the need to restore the good image of the colonial government that was damaged in proceedings at the European parliament following the Puputan War of 1906-1908 in Bali. The Puputan War was considered by Europeans as a massacre of an unarmed populace, so the Netherlands was keen on exacting a politics of "good will" by launching Baliseering, setting out to revive Balinese traditional culture and protect it from foreign influences that may otherwise spoil its authenticity.

The Dutch have been promoting Balinese tourism in Europe since 1914, initially using merchant ships to transport the tourists to the island. If there is any reason why Bali enjoys wider recognition than the rest of Indonesia, it is because they have been promoting it for more than a century.

Perceptions of beauty

Bali, as we have come to know her now, is actually a construct of cultural knowledge and beauty, planted in the days of yonder. Perhaps the neatest way of understanding decades of the island's transformation is to see it as a brand; Bali has gone through all the motions of branding that it lives on in the hearts of so many people around the world.

The journey of the artist Indah P. to Bali, for one, is inseparable from the course of history that has shaped the island over decades. Like many before her, Indah emerged in Bali with a wealth of preconceptions from a variety of sources. And even if she did not dip into the many studies and publications about Bali, she is bound to hear it from the more than 11 million people who visit every year.

Unlike other people, however, who visit Bali and return with visual mementos or a story to tell, Indah chooses to document her impressions through poetry and paintings. And now her beautiful memories can be read in an anthology of poems called *BALI The Journey in Heaven on Earth*. Indah's understanding of documenting does not stop at taking pictures for an album of memories, but instead tries to provide a personal impression of the many occurrences that mark her visits to Bali.

During a visit to the island in November 2017, for instance, Indah wrote the poem titled "Every Moment":

> *I have arrived*
> *in the Island of gods.*
>
> *The Island where you and I*
> *will treasure every moment*
> *in life ...*

This short poem is seemingly able to represent the emotions of so many people who set foot on the island for the first time. It was clear that Indah was happy that the Bali that had been living in her mind all this time was finally stretched out in front of her. It has become the reason why she believes every moment of life will be valuable. This is especially apparent in the next poem, "The Place":

This is the place
where I want to spend
my precious time

This is a shorter poem, but wades into the realm where Indah is certain she wants to spend all of her precious time in Bali. For her, the island not only becomes a locus, but also a strand that entwines the enchanting natural and cultural landscapes – that is why Indah does not want to enjoy it for herself. Have a read of the following poem titled "Together":

The soul of the sky sings in silence.
The colour of the sea is blue ...

I will explore the beauty of this Island.
Together, with you ...

On the next page, Indah felt the need to paint in the outline of the evening sun against the backdrop of gapura, umbrellas, *penjor* (ornamental bamboo poles) and coral rock. In its center she colored in the blue of the sea with steps leading up to the evening sky. The illustration, using watercolors on paper, called out to its beholder, as if to invite those who read the poem to ruminate on the beauty that has been conferred by the gods;

a fragment of beauty that can be found on her beloved island, the island of Bali.

Before we jump from the first part of her book titled "The Arrival" to the second called "The Wonder", the reader is guided along by a poem called "The Last Paradise" – an obvious nod to the movie that K'tut Tantri watched on Hollywood Boulevard in 1932. Despite using the same title, Indah sought to express how the last heaven on earth had become the place where she found her true self. In this instance, Bali had become a cultural landscape for reflection and self-discovery. The complete poem reads: // *This is the last paradise on earth / a hidden heaven along the ocean / Encircled by the temples / Surrounded by the sea / A place renowned for its serenity // There is nothing to worry / Because here, I will find my felicity / I will see a breathtaking beauty / of the island blessed by the deities / adorned with millions of frangipanis //.*

When we are all truly ready to enter Bali, Indah then shows us the magical facets of this sincerely beloved island. Her poems in the second part, "The Wonder", mostly recount Indah's experiences when she discovers Bali and all that she contains. In one instance, she visits a temple to view the Barong or Legong dances. One profound impression that she always repeated and eventually put to paper: "Every time I hear the music from the Barong dance, I immediately tear up," she wrote. In her poem titled "Barong Dance", Indah wrote: // *The sound of gamelan enters my heart / and tears begin to fall endlessly ...* // "I never understood why that happened," Indah added.

The temple, the Barong, Legong and Kecak dances, Mount Agung, the sunset, the stars and the full moon; they are for Indah some of the wonders of Bali that likely have no equal in this world. They are what she believes is part of the reason why Bali continues to be dubbed the last paradise on earth.

The following passages from this anthology are taken from chapters including "The Beauty", "The Love" and "The Memory". Undoubtedly the most prominent of all of these is when Indah notes of a memory in "A Part of Me". In it she writes: // *You have become a part of me / thus you will stay in my heart forever / Just like the moon shining bright in January / and like the stars glimmering in December ...* //.

Most of Indah's poems are actually personal footnotes that she tries to share with many people. It would be fortunate if everyone she touches is able to have a similar experience when they actually face Bali. At least the artists and researchers from the West, who came along long before Indah visited Bali, had a similar point of view. Most people view Bali from the lens of the culturally exotic, the perspective of Western Orientalists. But Bali harbors a wealth of (traditional) cultural riches that needs to be preserved because it is a piece of heaven that is left in the midst of rapid and globalized change.

The poems and paintings that Indah includes in this book will become a lingering impression of memory, because it will live on in the minds of many people. Consciously or not, Indah has upheld the memories written or etched by many creators before her. The most phenomenal has to be the meeting of Rudolf Bonnet and Walter Spies in Ubud in the early 1930s. The two of them had met the King of Ubud, Tjokorda Gde Agung Sukawati, and established a collective of artists called Pita Maha. This group would later give birth to the Ubud and Batuan style of painting, which subsequent artists inherited.

I am certain that what Indah has written will enter the vernacular and that this beauty will be preserved in the minds of many people. And these people will come to be the next "worshippers" of Bali. The poems in this book will further underscore how Bali's energy has been inexhaustibly sapped from all sides. Indah has carried out one important task throughout her artistic journey, and that is to share a deeply impressive beauty that fosters a universal love for culture.

In due time, everything will become a lingering impression of memory, one that is endlessly retold and passed down from generation to generation. Indah's works will be reproduced by her many readers, precisely to further strengthen the "branding" of Bali, that small island that enjoys wider recognition than the rest of Indonesia.

Putu Fajar Arcana,
literature editor of *Kompas* Daily in Jakarta.

The Arrival

Every Moment

I have arrived
in the island of gods.

The island where you and I
will treasure every moment
in life...

Indah P.
November 2017

The Place

This is the place
where I want to spend
my precious time...

Indah P.
November 2017

Together

The soul of the sky sings in silence.
The colour of the sea is blue...

    I will explore the beauty of this island.
    Together, with you...

Indah P.
November 2017

Indah P.

The Carved Door

Today,
I will open the carved door
to begin a journey I've never taken before.

I can feel it with my inner heart.
I can see it with my spiritual eyes.
Nothing else matters.
Serenity lies within myself.

Thus, the spirits sing
a song of a new beginning...
By being here, I will find the way
to be true to myself again...

Indah P.
October 2017

A Beautiful Place

It's the place
> where eternal waves
> crash onto the shore...

It's the place
> where dreamcatchers
> are displayed with
> their splendid shapes
> and colours...

You shall see them with your own eyes.
It's a beautiful place, a paradise.

Indah P.
November 2017

Your Spirit

This is a sacred island
surrounded by the ocean.
Protected by the temple
built on the cliff by the sea.

Bali,
your spirit lives within me...

No matter how cold life can be,
you will always be blessed by serenity
because you are the only place on earth
where I can feel the endless tranquility.

Indah P.
May 2017

The Last Paradise

This is the last paradise on earth,
a hidden heaven along the ocean.
Encircled by the temples.
Surrounded by the sea.
A place renowned for its serenity.

There is nothing to worry,
because here, I will find my felicity.
I will see a breathtaking beauty
of the island blessed by the deities
adorned with millions of frangipanis.

Indah P.
November 2017

The Sky of Bali

The light illuminates
      the sea with its glory...
I hope this moment will last forever
      for I don't want to forget
      this dazzling scenery...
The sound of the waves
      fills my heart with
      an everlasting symphony...
and together, we will realize our dreams
      to fulfill our destiny
      as we breathe
      beneath the sky
      of Bali...

Indah P.
November 2017

Indah P.

The Sound of Percussion

The sound of percussion
    awakens me from a deep slumber.
It enters my heart like the wind
    blowing towards the core of my soul.
Neither the mountains nor the spirits realize
    that the time of my revival has come.
All the nameless fireflies will call my name
    and the bright stars will rule the storm.

Across the ocean, beyond the sea...
    I have come to the island of purity...
And I will begin a new beginning for me...
    to create my own story...

Indah P.
September 2017

The
Wonder

Colours

On the beach of Padang Padang,
I gaze at the sunset with you.
Vibrant colours cover the sky
as felicity envelops this heart of mine.

This is a time of eternal wonder
given to us by the Creator...

The serene silence
and the inspiring moment
will become a memory
that will never be forgotten...

Indah P.
September 2017

The Meteor Shower

The sound of the waves
heals my broken heart
as the song of the moon
reminds me of you...

In silence,
I'm all alone,
abandoned on the shore
with a wounded soul...

But, under the magical sky
I can see the miracle
before my eyes...

It shows me the beauty
of the meteor shower
adorning the dark night...

Forever, I will always remember
the colours of shooting stars
in the sky of the island of gods...

For they are my treasures
falling from the heavens
where the light of hope
illuminates the entire universe...

Indah P.
September 2017

The Legong

Here I am...
in the center
of the universe.
Watching the Legong
with a heart full of wonder.

Nothing compares to this feeling,
for my heart is overflowing
with love and longing
as I'm enchanted
by the dance
before my eyes.

Indah P.
October 2017

Indah P.

Red and Gold

The music starts to play.
The dancers begin to dance.
Everything is decorated
with red and gold.

I'm captivated by the melody.
I'm mesmerized by the beauty.
My heart is encompassed
by red and gold.

Like the colour of the sun
and the colour of the moon.
I will never forget the charm
of red and gold.

For they are
the most
beautiful
colours
in the world.

Indah P.
September 2017

Dragonfly

A dragonfly appears in the secret garden.
Her wings carry the prayers of mother nature.

It's a wonderful thing to see.
For she represents the marvel of the
universe.

She lives proudly as she shows me her beauty.
She flies gracefully towards her own destiny.

It's a moment of joy.
A lovely scenery.

Indah P.
October 2017

The Mother Mountain

You are sacred
and very kind...
towards your people
living in this island...
for you are
the mother mountain...

You live in everyone's heart...
A part of nature
blessed by the gods...

I hope you will live in serenity...
because every soul
is praying for your tranquility...

Thus at this very moment,
I too, pray for you, mother mountain...
Because I know that you're alive,
as you are the spirit of life...

Indah P.
October 2017

Indah P.

The Sunset

I listen to the sea breeze
blowing gently from the ocean...

In silence, I gaze at you,
the sunset that I adore...

This is the moment of serenity.
It will last forever, for eternity.
No one can take it away from me.
Because it has been engraved on my memory.

You mesmerize me with your glorious colour.
It illuminates the deepest part of my soul.
You are a miracle given by the mother nature.
The one I always see before the nightfall.

Sunset, keep adorning the sea with your majesty.
For you're everything I want to see in this world of mystery.
Nothing compares to your glory.
I'm in awe of your magnificent beauty.

Indah P.
September 2017

Barong Dance

The sound of gamelan enters my heart
and tears begin to fall endlessly...

Sheltered by a thousand stars,
I can see the eternal battle
between good and evil
portrayed by the dance.

Barong,
you are the king of the spirits,
so powerful and glorious,
a sacred entity adored
by the believers.

Your existence
will be the light
within my heart,
as you have shown me
the courage and bravery
to protect the world
from the tragedy.

Forever,
you will always
live in my memory.
Never be forgotten,
for eternity...

Indah P.
November 2017

Kecak

Words will not be able
to describe this feeling
because all I can see
is a wonderful thing.

Love, sadness and despair...
Wisdom, power and glory...

Everything unites in Kecak fire dance
to show the world its eternal brilliance...

Indah P.
October 2017

Everlastingly

The grey clouds
shelter the temple of Uluwatu
where the voices echo
in the sky of my heart.

Beautiful and inspiring.
Soulful and breathtaking.
I am enchanted by the dance
performed before my eyes.

It will become a memory
that will never be forgotten within me.
A sacred dance in the island of gods.
Illuminating my soul.
Everlastingly...

Indah P.
September 2017

Dreamcatchers

Hundreds of dreamcatchers
with their beautiful colours
decorate the beach of Sanur
like snow crystals falling from the sky.

Such a wonderful thing to see
as they were made to be adored
because the spirits of dreamcatchers
are sacred like the wings of the angels.

So when one of them is given to you
don't ever let it go
for it will always protect you
and encircle your heart with hope.

Indah P.
September 2017

Indah P.

Garuda

The sun rises in the east
as the brave bird with his
unbroken wings flies with
pride and dignity.

He soars into the sky.
Courage and purity
are reflected in his eyes
as he is a celestial entity
created by the Providence.

    Garuda,
    you are the symbol of bravery.
    An immortal bird blessed by the heavens.
    A legendary being adored by humans.

    Living as a protector and a guardian.
    Ruling the air and the ardent flame.
    I will never forget your glorious name.

Indah P.
November 2017

The Song of Barong

Every time I hear this song
tears will fall from my eyes...

As the melody enters my heart,
I can feel the power of life...

It's a masterpiece of sublime beauty.
A song created with prayers and purity...

The song of Barong has touched me deeply
like the rain falling into the land of Bali...

Indah P.
November 2017

From Heaven

I can see the rain
falling down
into the ground...

The scent of earth
fills the air
in the garden
where I stand...

Even your rain
is beautiful, Bali...

It's like flower petals falling from heaven.
So sacred, just like the mother mountain.

Indah P.
December 2017

The Dancer

Your story is engraved on my heart.
Your movements are imprinted in my soul.

Dancer,
     you are the inspiration of life
     because nothing compares to your dance.

     It fills me with countless emotions
     as it shows me the path towards the source
     of imaginations.

     Indah P.
     March 2018

The Shards of Happiness

Billions of stars ignite my heart
as silence surrounds the temples at night.

My dreams turn into turquoise butterflies
blown by the wind towards the gate of paradise.

Within the darkness,
the candles flicker
like the lights of the angels,
as all the fragments of sadness
turn into the shards of happiness.

Indah P.
June 2016

Jimbaran Moon

The night is dark and serene,
the air is cold and windy...
Everything seems so distant,
just like my childhood memory...
but when I gaze at the sky,
I can forget the agony
because Jimbaran moon,
your light has illuminated me.
It envelops my fragile heart
with warmth and felicity.

Indah P.
March 2018

The Spirit of the Island

It calls out your name from the distance.
Like a whisper in the wind...
A soulful voice within a dream...

It tells you to come to this island,
to see the purity of the nature
that makes you want to explore further.

Blessed by the sky and the ocean.
Illuminated by the rays of the sun.
The spirit will live on
to protect this sacred ground.

And you will always remember...
because the bond between you and this island
is the bond that will never be broken...

Indah P.
September 2017

Like No Other

It's a place with a soul,
so pure like the ocean...

It's a place guarded by spirits,
so sacred like no other...

It's the source of inspiration.
It's beyond imagination.

It's the one and only paradise on earth.
It's Bali, the renowned island of gods.

Indah P.
March 2018

The Beauty

The Heart of Ubud

I take a deep breath
as I enter the heart of Ubud
     where green landscape
     welcomes me
     and natural splendor
     amazes me.

Indah P.
October 2017

The Emerald

It's the emerald of the archipelago...
So precious, no one can ever let it go...

It has many wonderful things to discover.
An island adorned with frangipani flowers.

It will stay within my heart forever...
A heavenly place to remember...

Indah P.
October 2017

The Frangipani

I remember the beauty
of the frangipani
blooming in the garden
at the temple by the sea.

The bliss
is represented
by her petals.
The dreams
are shown
by her colours.

The frangipani
is everlasting.
A gorgeous flower
with a deep meaning.

Indah P.
September 2017

Always

I will always remember...
      the sound of the tranquil waves
      at the serene beach of Sanur.

I will always treasure...
      my memory of the azure sky
      at the Ulun Danu temple in Bedugul.

Bali, your name echoes within me...
      For eternity, I will adore your beauty
      because you have called me
      to come here to see your glory...

Indah P.
November 2017

The Source of Inspiration

You are adorned
with the rays of the sun.
They call you the island of gods.
A renowned place on earth...

And nothing can surpass
the beauty of Bali...
For it's the source of inspiration
that will last for eternity...

Indah P.
September 2017

The Lotus

You're a lotus
      in the water garden
      where fireflies
glow in the dark.

You're so beautiful
      like the pouring rain
      I can see
through my window pane.

I want to
      gaze at you
      forever,
because your colour
      is magical,
      just like
      a timeless miracle.

Indah P.
May 2017

Protected

My Lord,
I pray to You
for the eternal serenity
and everlasting tranquility
in the island of Bali.

I believe in the power of hope
surrounding this place with its light.
Nothing can ever defile this ground
because it's protected by the guardians.

It will never be forgotten...
It will always be remembered...
And only the ones who're called
to this place
understand the purity of the mother
mountain and its grace.

Indah P.
October 2017

The Last Home

My dear, I have found
the place where I belong...

It's here, where I can feel
the serene wind blowing from the ocean...
It's here, where I can see
the sunset glowing gorgeously on the horizon...

Someday you will understand,
that my love for this island
will remain eternal...
just like an everlasting star...

And like a river flowing into the sea,
this is a part of my destiny...
Thus I will never leave this place anymore
because this is my last home...

Indah P.
November 2017

Ricefields

The serene ricefields
have become the source
of an everlasting tranquility
within my memory.

Wherever I go,
I can see
the colour of life
on the plain of Bali.

Quiet and peaceful.
Calm and graceful.

It's the place
where I can be
myself
completely.

Indah P.
September 2017

Indah P.

Galungan

This is the time
>> when the ancestral spirits
>>>> come to the earth.

The time
>> when we celebrate
>>>> the victory of good over evil.

So, come along with me
>> to see the scenery
>>>> in this sacred island.

We will be amazed
>> by the beauty
>>>> of Galungan.

For the streets
>> are adorned with
>>>> colourful ornaments.

We shall
>> never forget
>>>> this precious moment.

Indah P.
October 2018

Vision

...And You've shown me the beauty of dawn
  to revive this heart of mine.
    As long as I live, I will remember this vision,
  like an eternal dream of the legendary island.

...And this is the earthly paradise I've been searching for.
  It will not be forgotten. It shall be adored.
    Until the sea becomes a barren land
  and the sun becomes a frozen star.

Indah P.
November 2017

The Dance of the Butterflies

They are the symbols of rebirth.

Frail and delicate.
Beautiful and lovely.
Just like a kaleidoscope of colours,
they are cherished by angels in the sky.

One by one,
the winged beings appear
in the garden of the orchids
where you play your violin,
until I am completely captivated
by the dance of the butterflies...

Indah P.
November 2017

Indah P.

White Cranes

White cranes
on the rice terraces.
So wonderful
and pretty.

How beautiful they are
and how beautiful it is
to live and
to be free...

Their wings are strong.
Their hearts are pure.
Their souls are eternal.

And they live in happiness.
In this world of miracles.

Indah P.
November 2017

Coral Gardens

The moment when you see
the light deep under the sea,
you will be amazed
by the colours of the coral gardens
living and breathing before your eyes
to show you the magnificence of life...

Imagination turns into reality
as the shade of indigo shows you its glory,
adorning every corner of your heart
as if you are all alone in the universe,
only accompanied by the silence...

It's the moment of everlasting beauty.
It will always exist in your memory.

Indah P.
November 2017

The Night in Ubud

The night in Ubud is so magical
because although it's quiet and dark,
the stars are glowing beautifully in the sky.
They look like the ocean of crystals,
captivating my heart in an instance.

Indah P.
April 2016

Uluwatu

In Uluwatu, I can see...
 the sun showing me the beauty of the light,
 the moon adorning my heart with its fireflies at night,
 the stars guiding me to reach the edge of the galaxy,
 and the rainbow colouring my dreams with serenity.

Indah P.
April 2016

Crescent Moon

My dearest island,
you will always be remembered.

There's nothing else I can say.
You take my breath away.

And I will cherish everything,
all the bliss and the grief I've felt
when I sang alone at your blue lagoon
for I was enthralled by your crescent moon.

Indah P.
December 2017

The Love

Love Story

This is a love story
　　　between you and me
　　　　　and the island of Bali...

Indah P.
November 2017

Song of the Clouds

In the middle of the rice paddies,
we sing the song of the clouds.

Our voices echo
in the sky of Ubud.

Nothing else matters.
We will always be together.

Forever,
our souls are intertwined.

Indah P.
September 2017

The Beach

I am the beach...
    The place where you shed your tears.
    The place where you engrave your grief.
    The place where you leave your memories.

You are the sea...
    The place where I feel the breeze.
    The place where I draw my reveries.
    The place where I colour my dreams.

You are the place where I belong.
I am the place where you will return.

Together, we will always remember
the golden days under the summer sun...

Indah P.
April 2017

Indah P.

The Days

I will never forget the moments
when you took me to this place
to see the wonderful sunset
and to admire the beauty of life...

I will remember the days
when we created sandcastles on the beach,
when we buried time capsules beneath the sand,
when we watched the fireworks at Jimbaran...

I will always treasure
our times in Bali...
For this place is our sanctuary.
It's our home.
Our destiny.

Indah P.
October 2017

Once in a Lifetime

Under the indigo sky,
I can see your smile
as I follow you to the beach of eternal reveries
where our dreams turn into colourful memories.
It's a once in a lifetime experience
that I will never forget
because we paint our hearts on the sand
and no one knows about our secret island.
I can see the sunrise glows beautifully.
You can feel the wind blows gently.
Let's create our endless summer days
as we engrave our wishes on the waves.
We will be together forever.
This place is our Eden to remember.

Indah P.
June 2017

Felicity

Someday we will be free
as our souls will return
to the source of
felicity...

We shall fulfill our destiny
for our songs shall echo
beneath the starry sky
in the island
of Bali...

Indah P.
February 2019

For You and I

My life is written by the stars
flickering in the night sky
where dreams come alive...

My story is sung by the clouds
like an everlasting reverie
colouring this soul of mine...

On the beach of hope,
I gather the pieces of my memory
and keep them in the heart of time...

I promise to treasure these moments
and cherish this life
until love comes again
for you and I...

Indah P.
September 2017

The Moment

Let the fire
brighten the dance
on the cliff of Uluwatu.

Let the ardent flame
enliven the dancers like
a tale retold just for you.

This legacy will live forever.
A legend inspiring the world.
Not a shadow nor an illusion.
A story delivered from the heart.

Never forget the moment
when you see the Kecak.
It's an eternal love story.
It's the source of gravity.

See it with your own eyes.
Be amazed by its brilliance.
Let it become a remembrance
and a memory from this beautiful island.

Indah P.
November 2017

Indah P. 2018

Pura Tanah Lot

And I gaze
at the temple
built to honour
the powerful
gods of the sea
      as the bright light
      of the sun
      illuminates
      me.

In silence,
I can feel
the protection
of the deities
sheltering
the island
of Bali
      as they guard
      the sacred
      Pura Tanah Lot
      for eternity.

And my love
for this island
will never cease.
      Forever,
      it will exist
      to fill my heart
      with everlasting
      purity...

Indah P.
October 2018

The Beloved Island

As long as you exist,
they will always yearn for you
because you are the beloved island,
you live in the heart of your people.

Even if I'm just a stranger,
I will always protect you with my prayers
because you are the island I adore,
my most precious treasure, evermore.

Indah P.
June 2016

Sail Away

We're separated by fate
but we'll be reunited by destiny
for despair cannot tear us apart
as long as I open my heart,
I will return to your side.

So, I let the wind blow over the sea
because I will sail away to you
and nothing can stop me from reaching you
for I know that our love is true.

Indah P.
December 2016

Beautiful

The world is beautiful...

Filled with everlasting stars.
Embellished with glimmering lights and butterflies...

Beneath the sky of the island of gods,
the indigo sea sings the melody of life,
the grey clouds call the golden fireflies
to wipe away the tears falling from my eyes...

Indah P.
April 2018

Stars

I've never seen such lucid stars
like the stars in Uluwatu.

Every time I see them flicker
I always remember you.

You are the one I cherish.
A part of me that will never perish.

As long as I live
I will remember your name.

Under the starry sky,
we'll be reunited once again.

Indah P.
April 2018

Melasti Ceremony

It's a ceremony
    to cleanse the sin
    of the nature on earth...

It's a ritual
    to purify ourselves
    by acquiring the water of life...

And the world will be healed once more
    from its surface until its core...

And prayers shall echo in the sky
    until they reach the edge of the universe...

This is a symbol of purity
    as bad things of the past
    are thrown into the ocean...

This is a form of eternal love
    dedicated to mother nature
    from all of us as humans...

Indah P.
October 2018

Our Last Day Together

At the waterfall
    adorned by
    the rainbow,
I'm mesmerized
    by your
    presence.

        Today will be
            our last day
            together,
        for tomorrow
            you will
            leave this island.

But even if
we're miles apart
you know
that I will
always love you...

        As long as we are
        under the same sky,
        my heart will
        always be
        with you...

Indah P.
September 2017

The Memory

Precious Memories

It's time to leave
this wonderful place
but the precious memories
will live for a thousand years...

Indah P.
November 2017

Teardrops

Farewell, the mountains of Bali...
Farewell, the beaches and the sea...
Today, I will leave you...
but one day, I will return to you...

Maybe I can't stop my teardrops
falling from my eyes like raindrops
for I won't be able to see the sun
rising over your horizon...

I know I will miss you...
as I'm captivated by you...

For everything I see under your sky
is a blessing I can't deny...

Indah P.
October 2017

For You

You are the source of eternal happiness...
Encircled by the sea of diamonds...
You have released me from nameless illusions...

For you, I will live...
For you, I will die...
I'm amazed by your magnificence,
so much that I can shed the tears of life...

Although you're a million miles away from me,
Your name echoes within me...

Thus every time I think of you,
my heart is dyed with the colour of blue,
just like the colour of your ocean,
forever, adorning my existence...

Indah P.
September 2017

A Part of Me

You have become a part of me,
thus you will stay in my heart forever...
Just like the moon shining bright in January,
and like the stars glimmering in December...

I hope you will always be
filled with love and felicity.
For you are the source
of my beautiful memories.

Wherever I am,
I will always remember...
your glorious mountains,
your emerald rice terraces,
and your gorgeous beaches.

Even if you're so far away,
these memories will never vanish...
They will live within me...
Evermore, dearest Bali...

Indah P.
November 2017

The Nameless Tree

She is a nameless tree
standing alone on the cliff of devotion
where she can see the azure sky and glistening ocean.

At night she is illuminated by the dazzling moon
telling her the story of a distant island.
An island so far away beyond the horizon.
A place where all pure dreams are unbroken.

Thus the tree prays to be reborn as an eagle...
So she can fly towards that island in the future...

Then the waves sing her a song
and the tree falls asleep in silence...
Dreaming about the last paradise on earth...
It's her most beautiful dream to remember...

Indah P.
November 2017

Indah P.

Ngaben

And I dreamed of a soul
entering the upper realm
as they held the ritual
of Ngaben...

       And the sound of music echoed
       until the ceremony to release
       the soul came to an end...

It was a dream
of the sacred island
again...

       The island
       where my heart
       remains...

Indah P.
October 2018

Treasures

Only the memories
left in my heart
reminding me
of you...

They are the tears I shed
when I gazed at the sunset
on your shore...

They are the scattered seashells
I found on your beach
when I walked alone...

They are the feelings I felt
when I saw the full moon
illuminating my soul...

These are the treasures of mine...
    and I will keep them within me
        until all the glimmering stars
            dissapear from the night sky...

Indah P.
December 2017

The Mosaic

You are the most beautiful thing in my room.

Small and fragile...
Glimmering and stunning...

A pattern of colourful glass...
mesmerizing my eyes...

Every time I gaze at you,
I can remember...
the time I spent in Ubud,
the scenery I cherished in Tanah Lot,
the scent of the wind in Padang Padang,
the colour of the clouds in Batubulan...

You are my most precious treasure.
The memento of my childhood days
when everything was still as pure as the sun
shining brightly in the cerulean sky...

Indah P.
November 2017

Indah P. 2018

My Journey

The voices of the spirits echo in the distance
as I begin my journey towards the source of my existence.

My life has been illuminated
by a hundred moons
glowing brightly in the dark sky
where the angels sing an ancient lullaby.

Like a dust, I was blown far away
from the place where I was born.
But You have protected me
with Your divine guidance.
Thus, wherever I go, whatever I do,
I will always remember my origin.

And in the distant future, this soul of mine
will return to the heaven on earth.
It will become one of the stars
Illuminating the island of gods.
Shining endlessly just
like a ray of light.
Reigning the
silent night..

Indah P.
November 2017

A Thousand Stars

It's the island...
adorned with eternal frangipanis,
protected by a thousand stars.

It's the island...
filled with wonderful memories,
shielded by the prayers of life.

One day,
I will return once again
because the island
has called my name.

Across the ocean.
Beyond the horizon.

I will return
to the island
once more.

Indah P.
September 2017

A Song

Let me sing a song
of a place so far away...
It's in the center of an island
protected by mother mountain...

It's dedicated to you
whose heart yearns for a home
after going on a long journey
to find a place where you belong...

It's the place where the azure sky
embraces the turquoise sea...
It's the place where you can create
all the precious memories...

Someday...
Someway...
I will take you there...

It will be you and I under the rising sun...
Treasuring our moments until the end of time...

Indah P.
November 2017

Indah P.

BALI | The Journey in Heaven on Earth

Indah P.

Acknowledgments

First of all, I would like to thank God who has given me the endless blessings in the journey of my life. I am forever grateful for everything You have given me.

I would like to express my sincere gratitude to Penerbit Buku Kompas for publishing this book.

I also would like to thank Mr. Patricius Cahanar. I am truly grateful for your guidance.

Many thanks to Mr. A. Novi Rahmawanta, my editor. I really appreciate your time and effort.

A very special thanks to Mr. Putu Fajar Arcana. I am very grateful for your support.

Special thanks to Mr. Warih Wisatsana. I greatly appreciate your kind words.

My sincere thanks to Mr. James Luhulima. I will always be grateful to you.

Thanks to Mrs. Anna Wiksmadhara. I really appreciate your kindness. Thank you for everything you have taught me.

I am eternally grateful to my mother, Budhieningsih Sudono. You are my best friend and my hero. The brightest light in the journey of my life. I am blessed to have you as my mother.

To my father, Chandra Kemal. Thank you for all your help and guidance. I really appreciate it.

Finally, I would like to thank my family, all my friends and everyone who has given me the support. I am grateful to have met all of you. Thank you.

About the Author

Indah P. is a painter, songwriter and also a poet. As an artist, she has held painting exhibitions at Rumah Jawa Gallery where all her paintings were exhibited with her poems.

She graduated from a private university in Jakarta majoring in English Literature. She likes to write poems about life, hope, strength, happiness, sadness and dreams.

To know more about her, follow her on Instagram: @thefantasia.art